DYSLEXIA

ALSO BY ELAINE LANDAU

DYSLEXIA

BY ELAINE LANDAU

A FIRST BOOK

FRANKLIN WATTS

NEW YORK / LONDON / TORONTO / SYDNEY / 1991

Photographs copyright © : Photo Researchers, Inc.: pp. 13 (Richard Hutchings), 14 (Blair Seitz), 18, 19 (all Will & Deni McIntyre), 20 (L. Migdale); Robbins Photography: pp. 15, 23, 32, 40; Cameron Cudhea: p. 24; Landmark College, Putney, Vt.: pp. 25, 47, 49, 50; Dyckman: p. 27; Little, Brown & Co.: p. 34 (originally printed as fig. 3B of Galaborda, AM et al, Ann Neurol. 18:222–233, 1985); Wide World Photos: p. 42; Historical Pictures Service, Chicago: p. 44; Trevor's Campaign for the Homeless: p. 45.

Library of Congress Cataloging-in-Publication Data

Landau, Elaine.
Dyslexia / by Elaine Landau.
p.   cm. — (A First book)
Includes bibliographical references and index.
ISBN 0-531-20030-2
1. Dyslexia—Juvenile literature.   I. Title.   II. Series.
RC394.W6L36   1991
616.85'53—dc20   91-3139   CIP   AC

For T. J. P.—our duckling
who turned into a swan

CONTENTS

DYSLEXIA

1
MARK'S STORY

*N*o one doubted that Mark was smart. Yet he wasn't an ideal student. Instead, Mark had learned how to successfully dart his teacher's questions. Sometimes when called on in class to answer a question he didn't know, he'd try to say something funny. This served two purposes for Mark. He'd make his classmates laugh and cause the teacher to call on someone else.

As a small child, Mark seemed very much like any young boy. He was slower to speak than his older sisters, but later Mark managed to earn average grades in school. However, Mark had actually been more of an actor than anyone suspected. At times, he had fooled his parents, friends, and teachers. They didn't know that Mark was barely able to read or write.

Mark realized early on that he was different from his

classmates. It was especially clear when his teacher used the blackboard. Mark saw that everyone in the class could read what she wrote—everyone but him, that is.

Mark felt there had to be something wrong with him. His handwriting was sloppy and hard to read. His teachers complained about his poorly formed letters. Reading assignments were often more like torture than homework. Mark thought he was stupid.

School had become a frustrating experience for him. But Mark was too ashamed to tell anyone about his problem. He knew about the special classes given at his school. Those classes were for students who couldn't keep up in a regular classroom.

Mark didn't want to be different. He'd never wanted to be special in that way. He felt he had to hide the truth to survive.

As a result, Mark worked quite hard in school. But his efforts usually weren't directed at improving his grades. Mark poured all his energy into finding ways to cover up what was really happening to him.

He became an expert at learning to get by. Often he'd trick his teachers into giving him the right answers by making them think he had just forgotten what he was about to say. He offered his friends his baseball cards and opportunities to play with his Nintendo games. In return, they'd let him copy their homework and test papers.

Elementary school students point to countries on a map. Without special instruction, some dyslexic students have trouble reading maps and feel left out during classroom activities.

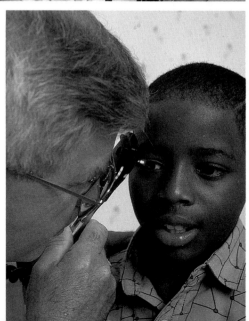

It is important to rule out any health problems before determining if a child is dyslexic. A young girl, above, has her throat examined, while a boy's vision is checked.

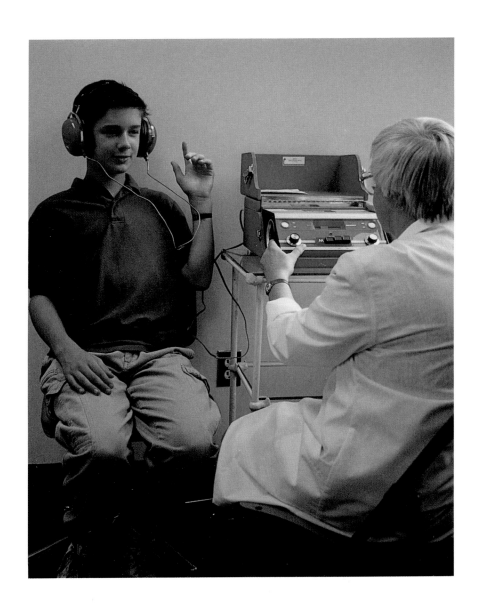

Here a boy takes a hearing test.

Whenever possible, Mark tried not to be called on in class. He'd sit slumped low in his seat. He'd stare down at his desk or papers to avoid his teacher's eyes.

Reading period was the worst time of the day for Mark. He learned to listen carefully when the good readers read aloud. Mark memorized their words as best he could. This system worked well enough except when he was called on to read a paragraph he didn't know.

Mark tried his best to keep his painful secret. However, as might be expected, after a time, he was found out. At first, Mark felt angry and humiliated. For years, he had hurt inside, believing he was "dumb." He didn't want to face the others at school if everyone knew.

Although Mark had difficulty reading, writing, and spelling, he was not stupid. In fact, testing later showed that Mark was extremely intelligent. His problems at school had largely stemmed from the fact that Mark was dyslexic.

2
DYSLEXIA

Dyslexic children often find it hard to identify printed words. Therefore, reading, writing, and spelling are frequently difficult for them. Dyslexic children may be able to understand a complex thought or idea read aloud to them. However, they may be unable to read it for themselves or write it in their own words.

For example, many dyslexics have problems remembering whole words. If the teacher writes a word on the blackboard and tells the class to look at the word and repeat it, the dyslexic student will be at a disadvantage. While the other students may later recall the word, the dyslexic will not. When classmates string together a group of words they've learned into a sentence, dyslexic children may not recognize many or

Here a young dyslexic girl tries a writing exercise.

If you look at her paper, you can see that she has trouble printing the words correctly.

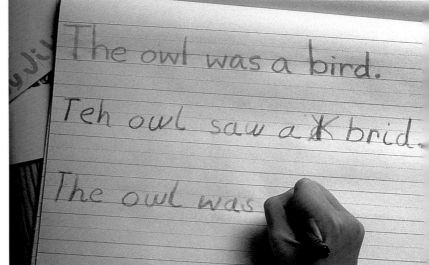

Discouraged, the student rests her head on the desk and tries to complete her work.

But realizing that she can't do any better without help, she stops trying.

Seeing her frustration, a teacher comes over to assist her.

*Try to read a book held up to a mirror
and you'll have an idea of the
difficulties some dyslexic students face.
But if a story is told aloud, as above,
these students usually have
no trouble following the plot.*

any of these words. This means the dyslexic will find it harder to read than most other children.

At times, after repeated tries, a dyslexic child may recognize enough words in a paragraph to understand it. Yet a few pages later, when some of the same words are used differently, he or she might not remember them.

Besides having problems remembering whole words, it may also be hard for dyslexics to remember individual letters. A dyslexic will often confuse such letters as *b* and *d* as well as *p* and *q*.

As one dyslexic boy put it:

There was nothing I hated more than reading periods. We had different reading groups in my class. They were named after birds—the Robins, Blue Jays, and Cardinals. Everybody in the class was in a reading group but me. I hated being left out.

The other kids knew that I was too dumb to be in one. It was awful. The teacher gave me other work to do during the reading periods. But I couldn't think about what I was doing. I felt too ashamed. I'd secretly watch the other kids in their groups. I'd just pretend to do my work. Sometimes, I'd see one of the kids looking at me. Then I'd really feel bad. I was always on the outside.

Writing can be as difficult for a dyslexic child as reading. Often dyslexic children will write certain words and letters backwards. The effect is like a mirror image. It is especially difficult for many dyslexics to write clearly in any case. Frequently, their letters are not properly formed. In addition, some dyslexics have difficulty transferring their thoughts and feelings into precise words.

Dyslexia affects various people in different ways. Some dyslexic people who have difficulty reading and writing speak beautifully. However, others have difficulty finding the right words to say what they wish. For example, a dyslexic child who wants to use paste might say something like, "Have you seen the _____, you know, the stuff you stick things together with?"

Although some dyslexics do well in math, others have problems with it. This may be because math is a language in itself. Frequently, dyslexic children reverse numbers in much the same way as some dyslexics reverse letters. They may not realize that 28 + 14 is not the same as 28 + 41. Yet many dyslexics who find math difficult are able to read and write with ease.

In some cases, additional problems accompany dyslexia. Some dyslexic children have poor coordination. They may not do well playing baseball or other team sports. One very young dyslexic girl found it hard to button her sweaters and coats or buckle her boots.

Dyslexic students who experience reading difficulties may be helped by special computer programs.

Although a number of dyslexics find sports difficult, this can be overcome. Here dyslexic students enjoy both winter and summer athletic activities.

Difficulty in distinguishing right from left can also be a problem for some dyslexics.

Many dyslexics have trouble being organized. They may scatter their possessions and then not know where their homework or other items are.

Dyslexic children who remain undiagnosed frequently live a waking nightmare. Sometimes in large classroom situations, these students slip too easily through the cracks. A teacher unaware of a student's condition may become cross with the young person. Often dyslexic children have been accused of not paying attention or of being lazy.

Yet all the while these students may be struggling to keep up with the others. Even as they fall behind in their work, they may be trying harder than their classmates to succeed.

Reading and writing are basic learning skills. They are the building blocks of knowledge through which other subjects are taught. A dyslexic child who is still struggling through a page of written material will be at a serious disadvantage when history, social studies, or geography is taught. He might be able to do well in any of these areas. But so much classroom instruction depends on printed words that his problem may limit his performance.

In many instances, dyslexic children have behavior problems. At times this may be partly due to the anger

Dyslexic students who have trouble reading may find other subjects such as geography difficult. These dyslexic boys do well in a small class especially geared for them.

and hurt that come from being unable to do what is expected of them. Often these students spend a good part of the day fooling around. They pretend that doing well in school means nothing to them.

On the other hand, the opposite may be true of other dyslexic students. They may spend most of their time just trying to pass. In any case, a dyslexic child who doesn't receive special attention will often experience a great deal of frustration. One dyslexic girl explained what she went through:

> You don't know what it's like. You want to be like everyone else, but you're not. And no matter how hard you try, you don't pick up things right away.
>
> I tried to write as neatly as I could. But my handwriting still looked like a little kid's. My teacher calls my work sloppy. She wants me to write more carefully. So now I sometimes hold the pen so tightly that my hand cramps after a paragraph.
>
> Once I felt really bad after a history test at school. I'd studied hard for it. I read the textbook as well as I could by myself. Then my older sister read it over and over with me. She's nice, and sometimes she has time to help me with my work.

There were four essays to write on the test. It took me a long time to read and understand the questions, but I knew the material. Yet it still didn't do me very much good. We had only one period to complete the test. I'd needed that long to do the first question.

I felt rotten. I knew I failed the test. And the horrible thing was that I knew the answers. I just couldn't get them out in time. When the bell rang, we had to pass the test booklets to the front of the room. But it was the last period of the day, so I thought there might be some hope. I told the teacher that I hadn't had time to finish the test. I asked if I could stay after school to complete it.

She said no. The test had to have been finished within the period. She said that's the way things work. Then she warned me to change. She said that next time I'd better get right to work and not dally.

There was nothing more to do. It didn't matter that I'd studied so hard. Like my teacher said, "That's the way things work." And I guess the large red F on the front of my test booklet proved she was right.

3
A LEARNING DIFFERENCE

It's been estimated that over 10 percent of Americans are dyslexic. The condition occurs among people of all income levels. There are dyslexics who are wealthy as well as ones who are poor. Dyslexia is also found among people of all races and religions.

Dyslexia occurs among people of all languages as well. A dyslexic child in China experiences the same problems with reading, writing, and speaking Chinese as an American dyslexic has with English.

Although no one knows why, dyslexia is more common among boys than girls. It's been estimated that nearly one out of every five boys is dyslexic.

Even though dyslexia was identified many years ago, it's a condition that has often confused researchers, doctors, and educators. Unfortunately, early on,

There are more dyslexic boys than girls.
At the Gow School in South Wales,
New York, a school for dyslexic boys,
students receive special help.

many dyslexics were incorrectly diagnosed. Often extremely intelligent young people were labeled mentally retarded. Instead of receiving help for their learning differences, they were frequently placed in classes for children with much lower intelligence levels than their own. At times, they were also placed in job settings in which they didn't belong. They were left to do menial, low-paying work when they were actually capable of much more.

Dyslexia is a condition that some people are born with. Dyslexics are usually of average or above average intelligence. However, they have difficulty processing information into language. The word dyslexia comes from a Greek word that means a problem dealing with language.

Over the years, the cause of dyslexia has remained rather a mystery. Scientists have a number of theories to explain the condition. Today many researchers believe that dyslexia is a result of the manner in which a person's brain develops. In most individuals, both the right and left side of the brain grow at about the same rate.

But this may not be true for dyslexics. Some scientists think that perhaps the left half of the dyslexic's brain develops more slowly. The left portion of the brain is the side that deals with language. Therefore, although a dyslexic may be exceptionally intelligent, he or she may still have difficulty reading, writing, or speaking.

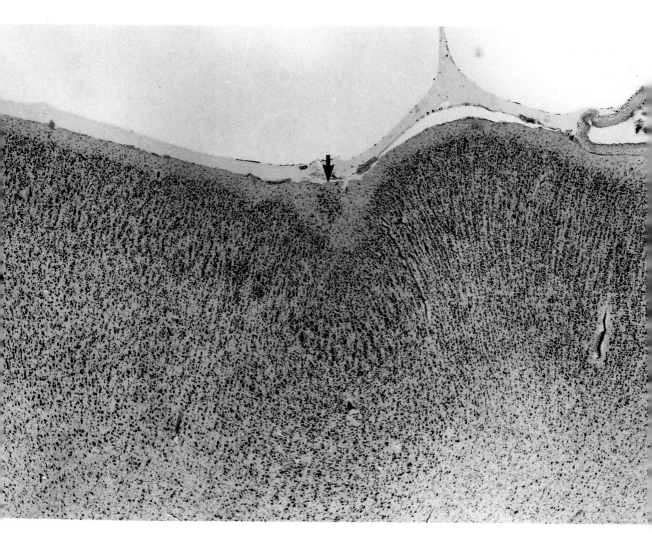

*In this picture of a dyslexic's brain,
the arrow shows a group of nerve
cells in an area of the brain where
they are not usually found.*

There are researchers who believe that dyslexia may not be a single condition. They think that what is usually thought of as dyslexia may instead be a number of separate conditions. According to this theory, different subtypes of dyslexia exist. Each of these would be characterized by varied symptoms. This would account for why dyslexia affects individuals differently.

A dyslexic who is not receiving special help may experience painful situations in other areas of life as well as in school. One dyslexic girl explained:

A lot of people take reading for granted. It's something they do naturally like brushing their teeth or opening an umbrella in the rain. But if you can't read, even the smallest choices make you anxious. The feeling is terrible. I'll never forget the time I selected a gift and card for my mother's birthday.

My father had planned a big surprise party for my mother. All our relatives were coming. The place would be swamped with aunts, uncles, and cousins. Everyone was bringing a covered dish. Since my mother had an August birthday, her party was going to be outdoors. It would be a sort of picnic party.

I'd saved my allowance for two weeks to buy my mother's gift. I went to several stores. I finally settled on a pretty flower-shaped pin. It was perfect for my mother. She loved flowers and spent a lot of time in our garden.

Then came the part I hated most. I had to buy a card. When I needed cards for other people, like Dad or my friends, I'd usually ask my mother to pick them up for me. I'd pretend that I didn't have time to stop at the card store.

I don't know whether or not my mother suspected the real reason. But if she did, Mom could be counted on to spare me the embarrassment of this chore. She'd usually say that she'd planned to go there herself anyway.

I couldn't ask my dad to pick up a card for me. He was always busy. And now with planning this party, things were worse than ever. I wondered if he'd even remember to buy his own card for Mom.

I spent about an hour in the card shop. That was nearly twice as long as it took me to get the gift. Reading greeting cards was especially hard. They tended to be wordy. And the print was often very fancy and hard to make out. So I had to go by the picture on the card.

I wasn't going to ask the saleslady for help. That would have been too humiliating. It's not like I came from a foreign country or anything. I wasn't going to tell a stranger that I couldn't read my own language.

I finally chose a card with what looked like a beautifully frosted birthday cake on the front. I couldn't make out the words inside. But I figured this had to be a good birthday card.

It turned out to be a disaster. My mother opened up her gifts and cards in front of everyone. I could tell that she liked my pin, but when she opened my card, she seemed embarrassed. My mother just said that everything was lovely. Then she put the card down and kissed and thanked me.

Unfortunately, my mother had passed all her other gifts and cards around for our relatives to see. My Aunt Beck grabbed my present and card, saying, "Don't hide the goodies from us." I felt miserable when I later learned that I'd bought my mother a card wishing her luck and happiness on her wedding day. The cake I'd thought was a birthday cake had actually been a wedding cake.

Later, while my aunts cleaned up, I overheard Aunt Beck say, "I feel so badly for Carol and Bill [my parents]. I can't imagine having a child like that." I didn't want people to pity my parents or me. It wasn't a good feeling. It just hurt too much inside to hear somebody talk about you that way.

4
OVERCOMING BARRIERS

*T*here is no cure for dyslexia, yet dyslexic children are capable of achieving a great deal. These students need to be taught by methods especially geared to their needs.

The techniques used to teach dyslexics vary. Different methods may work for various individuals. Some students find listening to books on tape as they follow along in their texts helpful. Often repetition proves useful in overcoming this learning disability. Some dyslexics have been assisted by continually listening to letter sounds and various combinations of letter sounds.

Educators are now aware that, if properly instructed, dyslexic students can absorb the same material as other

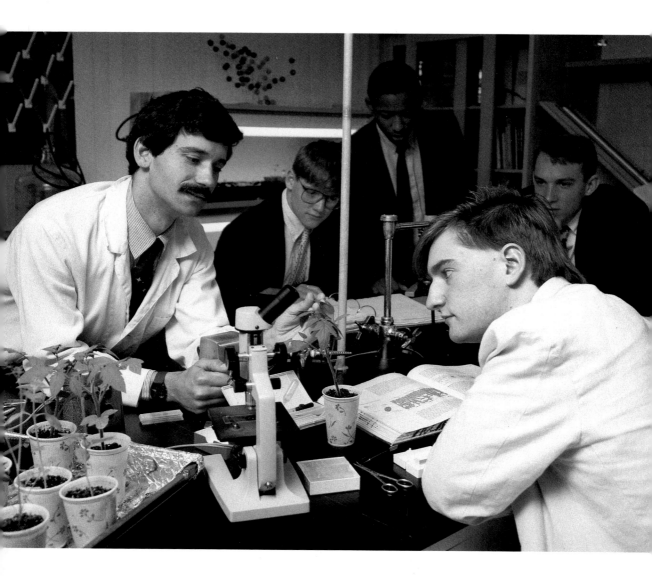

Dyslexic boys successfully work on a science project at the Gow School.

students. A dyslexic may have to work harder to succeed, but there's no doubt that he or she can achieve success.

Frequently, after they've mastered some basic skills, the confidence of dyslexic children improves. They may now feel able to take on new challenges. One young boy described his feelings this way:

When tutors or my parents used to tell me I was smart but that I just learned differently, I couldn't believe them. How can you think you're smart if you can't even read or write a postcard? But once I was enrolled in a special program, my feelings changed.

Nothing magical happened. Learning still isn't a snap for me. I have to spend much more time studying than other kids. But I don't mind. The rewards are worth it.

I think getting an A means a lot more to me than most people. It's positive proof that I'm okay after all. I know I'm going to make it now.

Numerous dyslexic individuals have achieved fame and fortune in various professions. Among them was the brilliant scientist Albert Einstein. Other famous dyslexics include former vice president and businessman

*Cher, the successful singer and actress,
is dyslexic. She wasn't able to read until
she was eighteen, and she didn't learn
she was dyslexic until she was thirty.*

Nelson Rockefeller; show business personalities Cher and Tom Cruise; and the wonderful storyteller Hans Christian Andersen. Writer Agatha Christie, former president Woodrow Wilson, and inventor Thomas Edison were dyslexic as well.

Some dyslexics have made important differences in our society. A notable example is a young man named Trevor Ferrell. In 1983, when Trevor was only eleven years old, a television news report showing the plight of homeless people in Philadelphia upset him. That night he convinced his parents to drive him to Philadelphia, where he gave his extra pillow and blanket to the first homeless person he met.

Assisted by his family, classmates, and friends, Trevor visited Philadelphia's homeless people often. Trevor and his companions brought food and clothing to people who were cold and hungry. Before long, Trevor's Campaign was underway. Through this program, more than a thousand people work together to prepare and deliver nightly meals to the homeless. A donated boardinghouse called Trevor's Place houses up to forty homeless people. Trevor was honored by President Reagan for his efforts, and has received more than sixty other honors and awards as well.

Although at times some dyslexics have felt badly about their poor performance in sports, there are individuals who've become outstanding athletes. Among

The famous inventor Thomas Edison was
dyslexic. In this picture, a friend looks on as
Edison conducts electric lamp experiments.

*Trevor Ferrell, the dyslexic boy who started
an ongoing campaign for the homeless, offers
coffee to a person who lives on the street.*

these are O. J. Simpson, Bruce Jenner, Carl Lewis, and Greg Louganis.

Ellie Hawkins is another dyslexic athlete. Even though Ellie is a small woman—just five feet tall and weighing only about one hundred pounds—she's an impressive mountain climber. Hawkins credits her mastery of this demanding sport to several factors. These include being organized, learning to pay attention to detail, and a tremendous desire to succeed.

Because of her dyslexia, Hawkins experienced problems playing team sports. In group games such as volleyball, there just seemed to be too many things going on at once. However, she found that she was able to excel as a solo athlete. Now Ellie Hawkins is one of the top women rock climbers in the United States.

Hawkins wants dyslexics to overcome the barriers they face. She hopes her success will encourage others. Ellie Hawkins plans to map out a challenging new mountain route that she intends to climb alone. She wants to name the route Dyslexia to show just how much can be accomplished.

Great heights have been reached by dyslexics in many other areas as well. Throughout the nation, various colleges and universities have set up special programs for these students. One such school is Landmark College in Putney, Vermont, where small classes and individual attention are an important part of the pro-

These dyslexic students at Landmark College in Putney, Vermont, benefit from small classes and individual instruction.

gram. Many dyslexics have earned advanced degrees. Often they've gone on to become extremely successful in their chosen professions.

Special schools also exist for younger students. At the Gow School in South Wales, New York, dyslexic boys develop important learning skills in an encouraging environment.

There are numerous success stories of dyslexics who have overcome obstacles on all levels. One young girl explained:

Last year my friend Lisa's mother took us to this wonderful old-fashioned ice cream parlor out in the country. She'd said it was famous for its unusual homemade flavors. Lisa's mother told us both to order whatever we wanted. But, unfortunately, there was a problem. It was my usual problem: I couldn't read the menu. However, I was used to faking it in restaurants.

My friend and her mother ordered the "Boysenberry Blue Bonnet" and the "Jungle Banana Safari Special." But when it was my turn to order, I asked for a dish of vanilla ice cream. I figured that was safe. A place like this had to have vanilla. And it was important to me to make my friend and her mother think I picked it from the menu.

*Landmark College students enjoy a
relaxing break between classes.*

A dyslexic girl at Landmark College gets the help she will need to succeed.

But as soon as Lisa heard me, she said, "You're kidding. You want vanilla. Didn't you read the menu? Look at the great things they have here." I wished I could have had one of those gooey treats. But the shame of having the menu read to me wasn't worth it. So I lied. I told them that plain vanilla was my favorite.

All that has changed now. Once I was finally diagnosed as dyslexic, I began working with a wonderful teacher from school. She really helped me. Now I can read menus and order just what I want. I'm not forced into being a plain vanilla person anymore.

APPENDIX

Organizations Concerned With Dyslexia and Other Learning Differences.

Association for Children and Adults
with Learning Disabilities
4156 Library Road
Pittsburgh, Pennsylvania 15234

Association of Learning Disabled
P.O. Box 9722, Friendship Station
Washington, D.C. 20016

Attention-Deficit Disorder Association
1387 Longdale Drive
Sandy, Utah 84092

Children with Attention-Deficit Disorder
1859 N. Pine Island Road
Suite 185
Plantation, Florida 33322

Council for Learning Disabilities
P.O. Box 40303
Overland Park, Kansas 66204

Learning Disabled Student Association
P.O. Box 447
Amarillo College
Amarillo, Texas 79178

National Center for Learning Disabilities
99 Park Avenue
6th floor
New York, New York 10016

National Institute of Dyslexia
P.O. Box 10487
Rockville, Maryland 20850

Orton Dyslexia Society
724 York Road
Baltimore, Maryland 21204

Perceptions, Inc.
P.O. Box 142
Milburn, New Jersey 07041

GLOSSARY

Decathlon—An athletic contest made up of ten different track and field events.

Diagnose—to identify a disease, difference, or disorder by its characteristic traits.

Dyslexia—a condition some people are born with, which is primarily characterized by difficulty with language.

Menial—low, humble, servantlike.

Subtype—a smaller division of a larger whole.

Symptom—a sign, mark, or signal that points to the existence of something else.

Theory—a proposed explanation to account for something happening.

FOR FURTHER
READING

Blue, Rose. *Me and Einstein*. New York: Human Sciences Press, 1979.

Gilson, Jamie. *Do Bananas Chew Gum?* New York: Lothrop, Lee & Shepard, 1980.

Janover, Caroline. *Joshua: A Boy with Dyslexia*. Burlington, Vermont: Waterfront Books, 1988.

Lewis, Marjorie. *Wrongway Applebaum*. New York: Putnam, 1984.

INDEX

ABOUT THE AUTHOR

ELAINE LANDAU has worked as a newspaper reporter, an editor, and a youth services librarian. However, she feels she has spent her most fascinating hours researching and writing books for boys and girls. Ms. Landau has written over thirty-five texts for young people. Her home is in Sparta, New Jersey.